ALL YOU NEED TO KNOW ABOUT BECOMING A SUPER SLEUTH

How to be a Detective

Paul Mason

GW00809133

Contents

World's greatest detectives wanted!

Are you ready to take on the challenge of a lifetime? The police need new detectives to join **police forces** across the country. It's a hard but highly rewarding job.

Just imagine the thrill of breaking up a gang of armed robbers, or chasing and catching a **suspect**. Your work would make sure people were safe. What better reward is there?

Of course, being a real detective isn't quite like on TV. Sometimes the criminals get away with their crimes. So a detective must always strive to make sure this doesn't happen.

So do you think you have what it takes?
Are you ready to test yourself?
If so, apply now.

Job description: detective

Being a police detective is an important job. Your work will be to identify, arrest and **convict** criminals. Successful applicants will have the following skills.

The ability to work as part of a team

Police detectives work with a team of other officers. Some are detectives, others are **patrol officers** or scene-of-crime officers (**SOCO**s).

Good people skills

You will need to be excellent at analysing both people and situations. Good listening skills will be needed for interviewing witnesses and suspects, and for communicating with other police officers.

Excellent eye for detail

You will examine evidence from a variety of sources, including witness statements, **forensic** evidence, interviews with suspects and **CCTV** recordings. You will need to analyse this evidence, to discover how crimes have been committed and by whom.

Of course, even before joining the police it is possible to start learning some of the skills that are needed to be a top detective. This book introduces some of them, as well providing an opportunity for you to test yourself to see if – maybe – you've got what it takes to succeed!

Becoming a real-life detective

Join the police

The first step to becoming a real-life detective is joining the police. After working in uniform for several years, officers can apply to become a detective. If they are accepted, they begin to learn the key skills of a modern detective.

These patrol officers may one day become detectives.

Becoming a police detective

1 When officers join the police, they attend a police training college or academy. They learn the skills of police work, from self-defence to understanding the law.

2 Next, they spend at least two years (usually a lot longer) in uniform, patrolling the streets.

3 Junior detectives work with more experienced police officers, learning new skills and procedures.

4 Detectives work in different divisions, learning how to investigate different types of crime.

5 Detectives may then be promoted to a higher rank.

Name: Ian Pollard

Job: Detective Chief Inspector (DCI)

Ian Pollard joined Sussex Police when he was 19 years old. He spent the next seven years in uniform. Ian says that these years helped him become a good detective:

"You get to know the people in the area, how they behave, the places where trouble sometimes happens. When you become a detective, information like that helps you to solve crimes quickly."

When he was 26, Ian joined the Criminal Investigation Department (CID). He worked as a detective in different departments, investigating a variety of crimes. Many people would find this hard, but as Ian says:

"The reward is helping make the city a better place for people to live. When we take a criminal off the streets, I can go home feeling glad."

Ian became a top detective, and today he's Detective Chief Inspector (DCI) in charge of the whole of Brighton and Hove CID. That means Ian's responsible for every case the detectives in the division work on!

Top Tip

Patrolling the streets is gruelling work and to join the police you have to pass a fitness test. The earlier you can start training to improve your fitness for the job, the better.

Gathering evidence

Police officers and SOCOs wear white paper suits and bags on their feet to prevent them from contaminating crime scenes by leaving their own footprints or fingerprints behind.

Key skills

Different kinds of evidence can lead to the person who committed a crime. Gathering together this evidence, and working out what it shows, are a good detective's most important skills.

Top Tip

Detectives have to be incredibly careful when examining a **crime scene**. They should:

1. Never disturb a crime scene until it has been photographed from every angle.

2. Never **contaminate** a crime scene with new material.

3. Divide the crime scene into an imaginary grid of 1 metre squares, and then search each one.

What to look for

Detectives use many different kinds of evidence in order to work out what has happened at a crime scene:

- **physical evidence** like a dropped wallet or mobile phone
- forensic evidence such as muddy footprints, hair or fingerprints
- witness statements, CCTV footage and records of telephone calls.

Detectives have to examine lots of different evidence such as this safe.

the safe door was blown off

Detective toolkit

Here are a few of the things a detective might need for gathering evidence:

- **Notepad** for writing down key information such as witness details
- **Tape measure** for checking distances, sizes and other evidence
- **Torch** for seeing in dark places, e.g. cellars
- **Camera** to record crime scenes
- **Sealable bags** for storing pieces of evidence
- **Magnifying glass** and **tweezers** for examining tiny objects
- **Rubber gloves** for handling evidence
- **Soft brush** and **grey dust** for collecting fingerprints
- **Evidence log-sheet** for noting down pieces of evidence.

It is important to make detailed and careful notes.

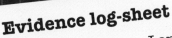

Evidence log-sheet

Location: Thames, London

Date: 01/04/2011

Incident: Valuable secret documents stolen

General notes: The room was in good order. Only the safe was disturbed.

Item number	Description/location	Comments
001	Small wall safe	Safe door open. Safe empty. No damage to safe.
002	Piece of checked fabric	Found caught in door – possibly from shirt sleeve.

Try it!

Test yourself by launching an investigation of your own kitchen. Who's been in there, when, and what for? See how many different pieces of possible evidence you can find.

Learning to recognise faces

Remember the look

Being able to recognise faces is an important skill for any detective. Detectives memorise the faces of criminals, so that they will recognise them later. Criminals often commit similar crimes again and again, so spotting someone who has committed a crime in the past often helps solve a new case.

shape of ears

size of ears

shape and size of mouth and lips

shape and size of eyes

distance between eyes

width of nose

angle of forehead

shape of nose

shape and angle of ears

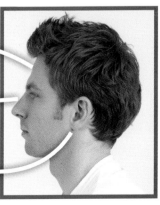

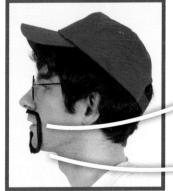

angle of mouth and chin

shape of chin

Detectives try to memorise many details of criminals' faces.

Seeing through a disguise

Of course, criminals know that the police might recognise them, so they sometimes disguise themselves. Skilled detectives can see through a disguise, by focussing on the parts of someone's face they cannot change.

12th November 2010

CRIMINALS ARRESTED WEARING "WORST DISGUISE EVER"

Two **burglars** wearing what were described as "the worst disguises ever" have been arrested by police in Iowa, America. The two men had been spotted trying to break into an apartment, wearing disguises they had drawn on their faces in marker pen.

When police officers went in search of the men, they found them sitting in a car. The burglars had been unable to remove their 'disguises', because they were drawn on with permanent ink!

Seeing through a criminal's disguise isn't always that difficult.

Name: William Merrilees
Born: 1898 in Leith, Scotland
Job: Detective

William Merrilees was a famous detective in Scotland. He was so small that he called the book he wrote about his life *The Short Arm of the Law*. Merrilees was a brilliant policeman. His most famous case happened during World War II, when he captured a German spy who was just about to escape.

Merrilees dressed up in all kinds of disguises while tracking down criminals: an old man, a sailor, an elderly lady and even a baby!

Of course, sometimes police need to wear disguises too!

Surveillance skills

Watch carefully

One thing many detectives have to do is go on surveillance. This means watching a particular place or person, in the hope that it will produce some evidence linked to a crime. Watching a place is called a 'stakeout'. Following a person is called 'tailing' them.

Sometimes police don't have to tail suspects. They can watch them on CCTV instead.

On stakeout

Detectives make careful records of everything that happens. They use a 'log-sheet' to make notes and take photos. The camera's time and date function records exactly when each photo was taken. At night, one of the biggest challenges is staying awake.

After long hours of nothing happening, surveillance can get boring.

These are just a few things someone on surveillance might need:

- Warm clothes
- Camera
- Surveillance log-sheet.
- Radio/mobile phone
- Binoculars

Surveillance log-sheet

Subject: Unknown male
Investigation: Illegal entry
Location: Thames, London

Date	Time	Officer	Activity
01/04/2011	23:47	GD	Suspect seen entering building wearing green hat. Face obscured.
01/04/2011	23:52	GD	Suspect emerges from building and climbs down fire exit, clutching something in right hand. Possibly papers or folder.
01/04/2011	23:59	GD	Suspect disappears into station.

Try it!

Make your own surveillance telescope. It lets you look through keyholes and under doors without being spotted. All you need is the smallest clear marble you can find, a sheet of thick black paper, and sticky tape.

1. Roll the black paper into a tube around the marble. The marble needs to fit tightly into the middle of the tube.

2. Tape up the paper so that the tube cannot come undone.

3. Push the marble to the end of the tube. Don't let it drop out! You need it to be poking a bit less than halfway out.

4. Stand in a corner looking out, and peer through the non-marble end of the tube. You should be able to see the whole room – upside down!

Observe and analyse

An eye for detail

At a crime scene, all detectives need good observation skills. This means being able to notice important details and also to analyse what these details mean.

To most people, this is an ordinary street scene, but detectives can use their observation skills to obtain lots of information.

The clock and shadows.
These show it's early afternoon.

Large buildings in background.
This is probably a large town or city.

Lots of shops and busy main street.
This place is popular with shoppers and other visitors.

Leaves on the tree turning brown.
It's late summer or the beginning of autumn.

Teenagers and children in casual clothes.
It's a weekend or school holiday.

Analysing photos

These observation and analysis skills are used when looking at photos and videos, too. Photos and CCTV footage can provide important evidence or clues. A good detective might spot that something has changed between two photos taken at different times, for example.

Name: François Eugène Vidocq

Born: 23rd July 1775

Job: Detective

Vidocq was a famous French detective. He founded the French National Police Detective Organisation in 1813, and the world's first private detective agency in 1834.

Vidocq was famous for the way he analysed crimes. He removed bullets from bodies to compare with those from a suspect's gun. He took a plaster cast of boot prints at crime scenes. Vidocq even tried to develop a successful method for using fingerprints.

Many books have been written about Vidocq's life.

Try it!

How good are you at spotting important details quickly?
Look at the photo on page 25. Study it for 15 seconds, and then turn back to this page. Now try to answer these questions.

1. Where was the photo taken?
2. What time of day and year is it?
3. Who is in the photo?
4. What are they doing?
5. What types of vehicles can you see in the background?

The more you get right, the better your observational skills!

Memory cop

Memory upgrade

Having a good memory for details is important for a detective. Even just remembering a criminal's name can be useful. Imagine hearing someone talking about 'the Whoosis Kid'. A good detective might think: "The Whoosis Kid? I know that name … didn't he **knock over** the Fargo Bank three years ago?" If there has been a bank robbery nearby, this information might turn out to be very handy!

All in the detail

Remembering details such as height, weight and hair colour can help detectives identify criminals more easily too. Here are some examples of how remembering the details can be important. Which description would make a suspect or witness easier to identify?

	Description 1	Description 2
Clothes	A dark coat	A long, dark coat, with a light-coloured stain on the left sleeve
Face, hair colour and eyes	A round face, with dark hair and normal eyes	A round face, with red cheeks and small, blue eyes. Dark brown hair cut very short. A little bit shaved out of his right eyebrow

Police use the details they gather to inform others of the criminals they are looking for.

WANTED

For Breaking and Entering, and Theft

Have you seen this man? He is wanted in connection with a robbery at 11:47 p.m. on 01/04/2011.

Sex: Male

Race: White Caucasian

Age: 25–30

Hair: Light brown

Eyes: Blue

Try it!

How good are you at remembering details? Study the picture of the person on the wanted poster for 15 seconds. Try to notice as many details as you can. Cover the poster and wait 30 seconds. Then try to answer these questions.

1. How old does he look?
2. What colour is his hair?
3. What colour are his eyes?
4. What is he wearing?
5. Can you remember any other details?

The more questions you answer, the better your memory. If you found it hard, don't worry. Just like a real detective, you will get better by practising!

The clue's
in the handwriting

Detectives often have to read written evidence. For example, they might need to look at witness statements, **confessions**, or ransom notes. A good detective gets clues from this written evidence – not only from what it says, but also from the way it's written.

Handwriting analysis

Handwriting analysis is based on the idea that someone's writing reflects their personality. It also shows how they were feeling while they were writing.

Size of writing
Big writing (over 9 mm high in total) often shows that someone is confident and outgoing. Small writing may mean someone finds meeting new people worrying.

We've got the plans you wanted to keep secret. If you don't leave I MILLION bills on London Bridge, we'll sell them to the unmarked highest bidder. You have 48 24 hours to make a decision.

Crossing out and additions
Show that the writer is confused or struggling to make a decision.

Pressure
Pressing down hard shows that the writer was serious, or angry about something.

Angle
Upright writing shows confidence and independence. Angled to the right = communicative, to the left = shy and quiet.

A matter of opinion

It's not only police departments that use handwriting analysis. Many companies also use it to help choose people for a job. However, not everyone agrees that handwriting analysis is useful.

View 1
Handwriting analysis is rubbish

"How can my handwriting tell you about me? I write in lots of different ways! Sometimes I write big, sometimes small. Sometimes I angle my writing to the right, but usually it goes off to the left. And the way my writing looks has changed at least twice in the last 3 years, but my personality hasn't changed at all!"

View 2
Handwriting analysis works

"Experts don't just look at one single part of someone's writing, such as size or angle. They analyse over 300 different features before coming to a conclusion. This gives them an overall picture of someone's personality. Analysing someone's handwriting always tells you something about them."

A handwriting expert could tell you what this person is like – simply by looking at their writing.

Fingerprint evidence

Prints of thieves

For a hundred years, since they began to be used in the late 1800s, fingerprints have been one of a detective's key tools.

What is a fingerprint?

The skin on your fingertips is covered in tiny ridges and dips. Look closely, and you can see that these ridges are arranged in a pattern. When we touch things, we leave behind a picture of this pattern. This is a fingerprint.

No Way!

Some police forces are now using ear prints in the same way as fingerprints! The shape made by someone's ear is just as unique as their fingerprints.

Fingerprint facts

Here are a few more fingerprint facts.

- No two people have identical fingerprints – even identical twins.
- Fingerprints are usually drawn in sweat from your skin.
- It's not only fingertips that leave behind a print. The palms of hands, and even the soles of feet, also leave behind a **unique** print.

Police and SOCOs dust for prints using a brush and fine powder.

Fingerprints and crime

In the early 1800s, detectives began to realise that they could use fingerprints to identify criminals. Anything the criminals had touched might have a fingerprint on it. Once uncovered, these could be compared with a suspect's fingerprints. This would show whether he or she had been at the scene of the crime.

Criminals often wear gloves to avoid leaving prints behind.

No Way!

In 1892, Juan Vucetich was the first policeman to solve a case using fingerprints. Vucetich's method of fingerprinting then spread to police forces all over the world.

Try it!

Imagine someone has taken something of yours. Maybe they left fingerprints behind. Here's how to check.

1. Shake talcum powder where you think the suspect has been.
2. Use a soft brush to spread the powder gently across the surface. Any fingerprints should show up.
3. Place a strip of sticky tape across the print, then remove it in one smooth movement. Stick the tape to a piece of clean, dark paper. You should be able to see the print.

Fingerprint identification

Match it

Once detectives have collected a fingerprint from a crime scene, they need to compare it with the fingerprints of any suspects.

These days, of course, computers do this. They don't just look at the suspects' fingerprints – they can also compare prints to those of every criminal on record.

Types of fingerprint

There are three basic types of fingerprint pattern: arches, loops and whorls.

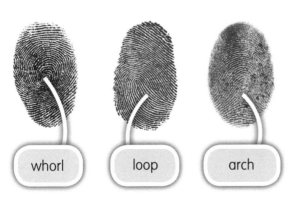

whorl   loop   arch

Detectives find it very useful to be able to identify the basic fingerprint types quickly. Imagine a murder weapon has a loop fingerprint on it, for example. If the detective knows that one of the suspects has whorl fingerprints, they may be able to **rule out** that suspect.

Different patterns

People don't necessarily always have the same kind of fingerprint pattern repeated on every finger. A person might have arches on their fingers, but loops on their thumbs.

Fingerprints need to be collected from suspects so they can be compared with those found at the crime scene.

Try it!

Once you've collected the fingerprints, you'll need to compare them with the prime suspect's. You'll have to take a print from every finger and thumb. This is how it's done.

1. Soak a sponge in dark-coloured poster paint. Make sure you use paint that can be washed off!

2. Draw a grid with two rows and five columns on the top half of a piece of paper. You should end up with ten equal-sized boxes.

3. Tell the suspect to press one thumb into the sponge, then press it lightly in the first box. Repeat with each finger, putting one print in each box.

4. Do the same with the other hand in the second row of boxes.

You now have a print of every finger and thumb to compare with the prints from the crime scene!

DNA fingerprints

A new discovery

Since the 1980s, a new kind of identification technique has become even more important to detectives than fingerprinting. This technique uses something called DNA. It can be used in the same way as fingerprinting, to show that a person was at a crime scene.

DNA is contained in the cells of almost all living things. It is tiny – far too small to see without a special microscope.

Sir Alec was knighted by the Queen for his work in genetics and DNA fingerprinting.

Name: Sir Alec John Jeffreys
Born: 9th January 1950
Job: Geneticist

Alec Jeffreys is famous as the man who developed DNA fingerprinting techniques. In 1984, he spotted that there were both differences and similarities between the DNA of members of the same family. He realised that if everyone's DNA was slightly different, then their DNA could be used to identify them in the same way as fingerprints.

DNA profiling

DNA profiling is examining someone's DNA and turning it into a set of numbers. Because everyone's DNA is different, the number their DNA produces is also different from other people's. The only exception is identical twins, who have the same DNA as each other.

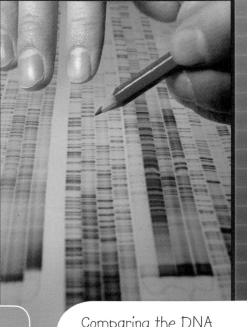

Comparing the DNA codes of different suspects.

Detectives have more chance of finding DNA evidence than fingerprints. Anything from a criminal's body contains traces of their DNA.

23rd January 1988

PITCHFORK CONVICTED!
First ever use of "DNA fingerprinting" in murder trial

Colin Pitchfork was yesterday convicted of the murders of Lynda Mann and Dawn Ashworth. Use of the new 'DNA fingerprinting' wonder technique played a crucial part.

Police were originally convinced that a 17-year-old called Richard Buckland had committed the crimes, but DNA tests carried out by Dr Alec Jeffreys proved that Buckland was not responsible. Dr Jeffreys said, "I have no doubt [that Buckland] would have been found guilty if not for DNA evidence."

DNA testing was then carried out on all the men living in the area. The tests revealed that local baker Colin Pitchfork was the killer. Pitchfork has been sentenced to life imprisonment.

Code words

Listen in

Detectives are always keen to listen in on what criminals are saying. As long as a judge gives permission, the police are able to tap criminals' phones to hear their private conversations. Detectives may even plant bugs to try and get evidence of crimes being committed.

Police on surveillance can also use long-range microphones to hear what's being said far away.

Criminal codes

Criminals know that the police might be listening, so they sometimes communicate with each other in code. This makes it hard for outsiders to know what the criminals are talking about. The code can be as simple as using numbers instead of words – for example, in the USA shouting, "Five-oh! Five-oh!" means, "The police are coming!"

Criminals use pay-as-you-go mobiles because they are cheap, disposable and untraceable.

Code words

Here are just a few of the hundreds of code words criminals use.

Angler: thief who steals by putting a fishing rod and hook through letterboxes or windows

Jumper: a thief who steals from offices

Twokker: car thief (from the police abbreviation TWOC, for 'taking without owner's consent')

Try it!

The simplest codes use numbers in the place of letters. Your code sheet would start like this:

a	b	c	d	e	f	g
1	2	3	4	5	6	7

Or you could start with the number 9, instead of the number 1. You could count up in twos, or backwards from 26.

Can you crack this code? Here's a clue to get you started: the first letter is 'a'.

2 / 24 10 20 6 / 14 2 15 / 8 10 23 6 20 / 15 16 / 4 13 22 6 20

The answer is six words long. Find out if you're right on page 31.

Body language clues

Spot the truth

One of the key skills for any detective is interviewing people. They may be witnesses or suspects. It's crucial to be able to tell whether the person being interviewed is lying or telling the truth.

No Way!

It is almost impossible to stop your body language giving you away – even for good liars!

Body language

Good detectives can judge if a person is lying from their body language, as much as their actual answers. Body language is a very powerful signal of what's going on in someone's head.

Arms and legs

How someone holds their arms and legs is a good guide to their mood. In general, when people cross or fold their arms or ankles, it means they are feeling defensive. There are lots of variations on this:

- holding a bag or papers tightly against the chest
- reaching across the body to touch, scratch or hold the opposite shoulder
- holding a drink in front of the body with both hands.

Eye movements

If someone looks to their right while speaking, it usually means they are lying, guessing, or making something up. If they look right and upwards, it is even more likely they are lying.

Looking to the left usually means someone is remembering facts, so they are probably telling the truth.

Mouth movements

If someone bites their lip, it may show they are tense, so does grinding their teeth or swallowing a lot.

When people rest their fingers or hand over their mouth, it usually means they are unwilling to speak.

Try it!

The next time someone does something like borrowing your bike and leaving it with a puncture, interview your friends to see who's responsible!

Ask the suspect to sit down opposite you.

1. Notice how they sit – is their body language defensive? Of course, this might be because they're worried about being questioned! More investigation is needed.
2. Ask if they did it. Watch their eyes – where do they look?

Interviews and confessions

Admit it!

Every detective loves to get a confession from a suspect. Even if there's lots of evidence against the criminal, a good lawyer might be able to get them off. But if the suspect admits to the crime, he or she is almost certain to be found guilty.

Making an arrest is only the beginning. As well as evidence, police often need a confession too.

This chicken criminal is clearly being defensive. I wonder what he is hiding?

Persuading a criminal to confess

If detectives think someone they are interviewing is guilty, they may try the following to get them to confess.

- Asking questions to which they already know the answers. The detectives are hoping to catch the suspect lying to them. This might persuade the suspect that it's time to start telling the truth.
- Presenting suspects with the evidence against them in order to persuade them to confess.
- Building up a picture that shows the suspect will be found guilty in court, and can expect a hard punishment. They then give the suspect a chance to admit the crime in the hope that the punishment will be less severe.

Name: Jay J. Armes
Job: Private investigator and police officer

When he was 11 years old, Jay J. Armes lost both his hands in an accidental explosion, but this amazing man refused to let this slow him down. He was determined to become a detective, and founded The Investigators, a **private eye** organisation. Jay J. went on to be a police officer and instructor for the El Paso County Sheriff's Department in the USA.

Jay J. also produced a detective course for children.

Good cop, bad cop

Detectives often interview suspects in pairs. They use a technique called 'Good Cop, Bad Cop'. The Good Cop is nice to the suspect, bringing drinks and being very understanding. The Bad Cop is the opposite. In the end, the suspect feels that the Good Cop is a friend, who can be told the truth about what happened.

It's not only the police that play Good Cop, Bad Cop!

Could you make it?

This quiz will let you test yourself on what you've learned from this book. It may also tell you whether you've got what it takes to become a top detective one day.

1

Your best friend puts on a scary fancy dress costume. When they turn up on your doorstep, how do you react?

A   Look at their eyes, nose and mouth and recognise them immediately.

B   Think they look familiar but you're not sure who they are.

C   Shout "AAAAAAAAAhhhhhhh! Help! Help!" as you run up the stairs and lock yourself in your room.

2

You have lost your trainers again. What do you do?

A   Carefully search each room they might have been lost in, starting with the one where you last remember having them.

B   Have a quick look in all the rooms in the house, five times, then shout for help.

C   Shout for someone to tell you where they are.

3

You got a big box of chocolates for your birthday but someone keeps eating them. What action do you take?

A Go on stakeout and keep a log-sheet of everyone entering your room.

B Watch your room for a couple of hours but then get bored.

C Hide your chocolates and hope no one finds them.

4

You're on a school trip when someone goes missing. What do you tell your teacher?

A Exactly what they were wearing and what they look like.

B What they were wearing but you don't remember all the details.

C That the person is nice but you can't remember much about them.

5

Someone has broken your favourite game. What do you do?

A Question all the possible suspects and study them carefully.

B Go straight to the person you think did it and question them.

C Go straight to the person you think did it and accuse them.

How did you do?

Mostly As
You have what it takes to become a super-sleuth! The police will probably be very pleased to hear from you if you decide to join them.

Mostly Bs
On the right track. You have some of the skills it takes but you need to work harder before the job is yours.

Mostly Cs
A lot of work to do. You'd probably make a pretty defective detective! (Either that or you took the quiz before you read the book.) Perhaps you might like to consider an alternative career?

Answer to Try it! on page 25.
A WISE MAN GIVES NO CLUES. The code starts with a being 2, b being 3, c being 4, and so on.

Glossary

burglar thief who enters a building with intent to steal

CCTV closed-circuit television: video camera system

confession admission that you did something

contaminate make useless by mixing in new materials

convict find guilty of a crime

crime scene place where a crime has taken place

forensic describes use of science to help solve a crime

knock over criminal code for an armed robbery

patrol officer police officer who spends his or her time on the streets, either on foot or in a car

physical evidence items at the scene of a crime that may help solve it

police force group of police officers working in same area

prime suspect person most likely to have committed a crime

private eye detective who is not a police officer

rule out decide not to include

SOCO "Scene-Of-Crime Officer": police officer who carries out forensic work at crime scenes

suspect person whom detectives think may have committed a crime

unique different from any other

Index